D1088461

LA LLORONA

THE LEGENDARY WEEPING WOMAN OF MEXICO

──◇◆ BY MEGAN COOLEY PETERSON ◆◇──

CAPSTONE PRESS
a capstone imprint

Snap Books are published by Capstone Press
1710 Roe Crest Drive, North Mankato, Minnesota 56003
www.capstonepub.com

Copyright © 2020 by Capstone Press, a Capstone imprint

Library of Congress Cataloging-in-Publication Data
Names: Peterson, Megan Cooley, author.
Title: La Llorona : the legendary weeping woman of Mexico /
by Megan Cooley Peterson.
Other titles: Llorona
Description: North Mankato, Minnesota : Snap Books, an imprint of Capstone
Press, [2020] | Series: Snap. Real-life ghost stories | Audience: Ages:
8-14. | Includes bibliographical references and index.
Identifiers: LCCN 2018058064| ISBN 9781543573374 (hardcover) | ISBN
9781543574791 (pbk.) | ISBN 9781543573466 (ebook PDF)
Subjects: LCSH: Llorona (Legendary character)—Juvenile literature. | Mexican
Americans—Folklore—Juvenile literature. | Ghost stories.
Classification: LCC GR114 .P47 2020 | DDC 398.20972—dc23
LC record available at https://lccn.loc.gov/2018058064

Editorial Credits
Eliza Leahy, editor; Brann Garvey, designer; Tracy Cummins, media researcher;
Tori Abraham, production specialist

Photo Credits
Alamy: Chris Hellier, 27, Chronicle, 21; Bridgeman Images: Museo Nacional de Antropologia,
Mexico City, Mexico/De Agostini Picture Library/Archivio J. Lange, 9; iStockphoto: Bassador, 13,
urbazon, 7; Newscom: akg-images, 29, Doug Meszler/Splash News, 23; Shutterstock: andreiuc88,
19, avtk, Design Element, Chantal de Bruijne, Design Element, Dmitry Laudin, Cover, Fer Gregory,
10, Giraphics, Design Element, GoMixer, Design Element, Lario Tus, 15, 16, 25, MagicDogWorkshop,
Design Element, NikhomTreeVector, Design Element, NinaMalyna (frame), 21, Prokrida (frame), 10,
11, 19, 28 Right, 28 Left, Tom Tom, 5, Yupa Watchanakit, 11

Direct Quotations
Pages 12–14: Radford, Benjamin. *Mysterious New Mexico: Miracles, Magic, and Monsters in the Land of Enchantment.* Albuquerque: University of New Mexico Press, 2014, 225–226.

Page 17: https://truehorrorstoriesoftexas.com/beautiful-ghost-lady-santa-maria-texas/

Pages 18–19: Radford, Benjamin. *Mysterious New Mexico: Miracles, Magic, and Monsters in the Land of Enchantment.* Albuquerque: University of New Mexico Press, 2014, 234–235.

All internet sites appearing in front and back matter were available and accurate when this book
was sent to press.

Printed in the United States of America.
PA70

TABLE OF CONTENTS

BEWARE THE WEEPING WOMAN

It's late at night, and you're roasting marshmallows with your family at a campsite beside a river. The flames crackle. Moonlight glints off the rushing water. Suddenly you hear a woman cry out for her lost children. But you don't see anyone. As you explore the riverbank, a woman in white drifts toward you. Her feet don't touch the ground. You scream, and she vanishes. Were your eyes playing tricks on you? Or did you just encounter La Llorona, the weeping woman of Mexico?

FACT

La Llorona means "weeping woman" in Spanish.

The story of La Llorona began sweeping through Mexico in the 1500s. According to the tale, a local woman drowned her children. Filled with regret and overtaken by heartache, the woman searched for her children up and down the river. She didn't stop her search even to eat or drink, and she died. Her spirit was doomed to roam the earth forever, calling out for her lost children.

La Llorona's story is still told today. Many people say the weeping woman is not a legend at all but a real ghost. **Skeptics** say that sightings of La Llorona can be explained by mist or lights. They believe there is no ghostly woman in white. Turn the page and decide for yourself.

CHAPTER ONE

THE LEGEND OF LA LLORONA

The legend of La Llorona has terrified listeners for hundreds of years. There is no single story of La Llorona. The most common version involves a beautiful **peasant** woman. When her husband dies, the woman must raise their children alone. She meets a wealthy man and falls in love. But the man doesn't want to help raise her children. He won't marry her.

Desperate to be with the man she loves, the woman takes her children to the river and drowns them. But after killing them, she dies from a broken heart.

FACT

The story of La Llorona is sometimes told to keep children from misbehaving. Parents warn their children that if they're not careful, La Llorona will get them.

The woman's story doesn't end with her death. Her spirit roams rivers and other bodies of water as she searches for her dead children. Dressed all in white, she cries out for them. Any children who are careless near water are snatched away by La Llorona's tormented ghost.

SKEPTIC'S NOTE

No child **abductions** have ever been tied to La Llorona or a ghost. If they happened as frequently as reported, there would be **evidence**.

TALES FROM MEXICO

Other versions of La Llorona's legend have spread throughout Mexico. In one story, a poor woman is left by the man she loves. She becomes depressed. While her sons sleep, she kills them. Then she takes her own life. Her ghost wanders the city streets at night, crying out, "¡Mis hijos! My sons!"

In another version, a mother drowns her children in a canal. No one knows why she kills her children. Her ghost wears all white and roams the city streets at night. She cries out for her dead children before disappearing into the darkness.

La Llorona is also said to haunt Mexico's **highlands**. At dusk, she appears to men returning from working in the fields. She calls to them in the voices of their wives or girlfriends. La Llorona leads the men to the edges of cliffs. Any man who follows her ghostly cries is pushed off the cliff to his death.

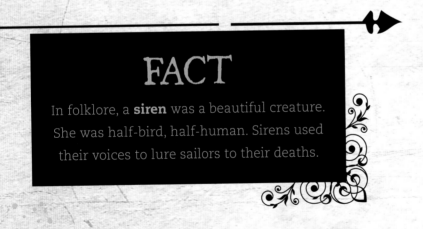

FACT

In folklore, a **siren** was a beautiful creature. She was half-bird, half-human. Sirens used their voices to lure sailors to their deaths.

The fearsome Aztec goddess Cihuacoatl is often associated with birth, death, and war.

CIHUACOATL

Some scholars say La Llorona is based on the **Aztec** goddess Cihuacoatl. The Aztecs lived in present-day Mexico long before the Spanish arrived. According to legend, Cihuacoatl stole infants and killed them. Dressed in white, she drifted along the streets after she killed them, wailing. Her cries warned of wars and misery.

LA LLORONA HAUNTS THE UNITED STATES

Mexican immigrants brought the tale of La Llorona with them to the southwestern United States. Like in Mexico, there are many U.S. versions of her story. Some say her children can be seen wandering the streets at night. Other tales say that La Llorona isn't a ghost at all—she's alive and bloodthirsty.

In another twist on the legend, La Llorona doesn't kill her children. On a cold night, she decides to leave her husband. She hides her children under a bridge on the shore of a river. Then she goes home to pack their belongings. But when she returns, the children have frozen to death. She haunts the river, weeping for her children.

FACT

In New Mexico, La Llorona's soul is sometimes associated with flames or balls of fire.

FOLKTALES AND URBAN LEGENDS

Folktales have been told for thousands of years. They are stories or legends passed from person to person. Urban legends are modern versions of folktales shared by word of mouth and online. Urban legends can be strange or scary— or both. They often deal with real-life fears, such as drowning or talking to strangers. Urban legends sometimes contain a lesson by telling us what *not* to do.

CHAPTER TWO

ENCOUNTERS WITH LA LLORONA

Is La Llorona a legend or a real ghost? Some people claim to have come face-to-face with the weeping woman. These real-life encounters will send chills up your spine. But are they enough to convince you she's more than just a scary story?

WALKING ON WATER

In 1931, a girl named Guadalupe visited the Santa Fe River in New Mexico with her two brothers. The boys spent the summer afternoon splashing in the cool water. Guadalupe played on the riverbank. Suddenly, a gust of wind tore through the river valley. It rattled the weeds and cattails where Guadalupe played. Then she heard the sound of tinkling bells.

SKEPTIC'S NOTE

Some skeptics say people mistake fog or shadows for La Llorona. People who "hear" the ghost are actually hearing howling animals or blowing wind.

Guadalupe tried to move, but she found herself paralyzed. "I could not move a muscle," she later recalled. "I was mesmerized by the sound of the bells for at least a minute." Once the sound of the bells died away, Guadalupe heard a woman crying: "*Mija, mija.* My daughter, my daughter." Finally able to move, Guadalupe and her brothers ran all the way home. Guadalupe's brothers also heard the woman calling out. But they heard her crying for her sons, not her daughter.

Guadalupe and her brothers recounted their tale to their parents. Guadalupe's mother whispered to her father, "La Llorona!" The family quickly returned to the river to see if they could find her. The woman could still be heard wailing. Guadalupe's mother shouted, "Leave my children alone, daughter of the devil!"

As the family turned to leave, one of Guadalupe's brothers yelled for them to stop. He pointed to the river. A ghostly figure walked on the water, her arms outstretched. The family fled in terror.

FROZEN WITH FEAR

Between 2000 and 2009, a young boy was visiting family in Durango, Mexico. He played outside with his cousins late at night. Suddenly, the boy found himself separated from his family. The hairs on the back of his neck stood up straight. The boy could feel something—or someone—watching him. When the boy heard the laughter of unfamiliar children, he became paralyzed with fear.

SKEPTIC'S NOTE

When faced with danger, people experience a fight-or-flight response. Scientists say that people often freeze while deciding whether to fight or run away.

Soon the laughter died out, and a woman began to wail. She begged for her children to return to her. Fearing it was La Llorona, the boy was finally able to move. He ran into his grandmother's house. Everyone inside the house had also heard the woman's cries. Was it La Llorona? Or is there another explanation?

FACT

In Santa Fe, New Mexico, La Llorona is said to haunt the Public Employees Retirement Association building near the Santa Fe River. Employees have heard wailing in the halls. Others report being pushed by unseen hands.

THE GHOST WITHOUT EYES

Two brothers in Texas got the fright of a lifetime near the city of Peñitas in the mid-2010s. They were driving home in separate cars on Military Road around midnight. This **barren** road runs along the Rio Grande River. As darkness settled, the brothers noticed a woman walking along the side of the road. She wore a long, white dress and no shoes. And she was soaking wet.

Concerned for her safety, the brother in the front car slowed down to ask her if she needed a ride home. The pale woman slowly turned toward the car. Her face was unlike any he had ever seen. She had gaping black holes where her eyes should be. The man sped away in his car. When he glanced in the rearview mirror, she was gone. His brother in the rear car also could not see her once he passed.

SKEPTIC'S NOTE

If the man pulled up next to the woman, his car's headlights would not have been pointing at her. Her eyes may have been simply hidden in shadow.

WHAT'S YOUR NAME?

Around this same time in Santa Maria, Texas, a young girl rode her bike to her cousin's house late at night. Her cousin lived near a cemetery close to the Rio Grande River. Just as she parked her bike in the driveway, a woman in white appeared. She hovered above the ground. Then the woman floated toward the girl, who was frozen in shock. Finally the woman asked, "Who are you?" The girl managed to answer with a fake name before running into the house. When she looked back, the mysterious woman had vanished. Had the girl spoken to La Llorona?

FACT

In some tales, La Llorona is 9 feet (2.7 meters) tall. In others, her face is a bare skull.

THE GHOSTLY HITCHHIKER

A winter's drive home turned into a nightmare for one man from Pecos, New Mexico. He was driving home late one night in 1953. His car's headlights lit up a woman standing alone on the side of the road. She wore a long, black cloak that covered most of her face. The man pulled over and opened the passenger's door. "Would you like a ride home?" he asked. The woman climbed into the car without answering.

As the man drove, the woman sat still as a statue. She kept one hand on her knee and the other inside her cloak. The man still couldn't make out her face. He tried to ask her questions, but she refused to utter a single word. Soon, the man began to smell **sulfur**. Nervous, he pulled the car over to ask her to get out. But when he turned toward his silent passenger, she was gone. The woman had never even opened the door to get out. Before the man could drive away, a **bloodcurdling** scream pierced the car's interior. The hairs on his neck stood straight up.

The man later told his friend what he had experienced. His friend had a shocking story of his own—he had also encountered the mysterious woman. "That was La Llorona!" said the man's friend. Even though the ghostly hitchhiker wore all black, the men believed the woman could be none other than La Llorona.

THE VANISHING HITCHHIKER

The Vanishing Hitchhiker is one of the best-known urban legends. It is told all over the world. In most versions, a driver sees a person on the side of the road. The driver offers them a ride. While driving, the driver notices the hitchhiker has vanished. The driver learns later that this person had already died. Sometimes the hitchhiker leaves something behind, like a jacket or footprint.

CHAPTER THREE

LADIES IN WHITE AROUND THE WORLD

La Llorona isn't the only ghostly woman in white. "White lady" ghost stories have been told around the world for hundreds of years. People use these stories to help them deal with and understand death.

BANSHEES

The banshee is a female spirit from Irish folklore. According to legend, banshees can be heard wailing at night. In Ireland, they are considered messengers of death. If a person hears a banshee's cries, someone in their family is doomed to die.

Like La Llorona, banshees are often said to wear all white. They are typically described as old women with long, white hair. They have red-rimmed eyes from crying so much.

FACT

Like La Llorona, banshees are often associated with bodies of water. In Irish **mythology**, water is a gateway to the underworld.

Banshees are common in Scottish folklore. In Scotland, a banshee-like being is known as *bean-nighe*. They are said to be found near rivers.

FACT

The White Lady is one of the Philippines' most famous ghosts. Sightings of her are often reported on Balete Drive in Manila. She is said to haunt cab drivers.

HAUNTED FRANCE

Ghostly women in white are also said to haunt France. Some haunt bridges, ravines, roads, and creeks. Travelers who want to pass must show respect to the ghost. According to some legends, the ghost extends her hand, asking for a dance. She lets travelers pass if they dance with her. But if the traveler refuses, the lady in white flings them into a ditch filled with thorns. Some ladies in white have **familiars**, or animals under their control. If a traveler doesn't show respect, the ghost commands her familiars to attack them.

FACT

In France, the white lady ghost is sometimes called *La Dame Blanche*.

WHITE LADY AT THE LAKE

In Rochester, New York, a ghostly figure dressed in white haunts Durand Eastman Park. According to legend, a mother and daughter lived in the area in the early 1800s. One night, the daughter went for a walk on the beach of Lake Ontario. She never returned.

Her mother searched the beach and surrounding woods for the rest of her life. Even after the mother died, her spirit never gave up her search. On misty nights, a ghostly woman in white has been spotted floating over the waves.

A storm ripped through Durand Eastman Park, and a strange figure emerged in the bark of a tree that had been damaged by wind. Some people believe this figure to be the ghost of the White Lady.

GERMANY'S LADIES IN WHITE

One of the earliest-known lady in white stories came from Germany in the mid-1400s. German white lady ghosts are called *die weisse Frau. Die weisse Frau* means "the white lady" in German. Some scholars believe this story was carried to Mexico by Spanish explorers. It may have inspired the tale of La Llorona.

According to the German story, a rich man died. He left behind a **widow** and two children. His widow hoped to remarry and soon drew the attention of a wealthy man. But the man said he would not marry her because "four eyes" were in the way. The widow assumed he meant the "four eyes" of her children. While her children slept one night, she crept into their bedroom and killed them.

When the man found out the widow had murdered her children, he rejected her. The "four eyes" he had referred to were those of his parents. They did not approve of the widow. The widow later opened a **convent** and became a nun. After her death, she haunted the convent. Her ghostly **apparition** signaled death to anyone unlucky enough to see her.

A MURDEROUS GHOST

In another German white lady tale, a young peasant girl meets a rich man. They have a baby together, but the man won't marry her. In a rage, the woman kills the man and their child. She is arrested and locked away, and after a short time she goes insane and dies. Her ghost wears a long, white gown. Anyone who speaks to this white lady dies within a few days.

CHAPTER FOUR

WAS LA LLORONA A REAL PERSON?

The tale of La Llorona has been told for hundreds of years in Mexico and the southwestern United States. Her story warns children to be safe around water. It also teaches parents to look after their children. But could La Llorona have been a real woman?

Some believe La Llorona may be the ghost of a native Mexican woman named La Malinche. In the early 1500s, Spanish explorer Hernán Cortés sailed to Mexico. He wanted to take the land from the Aztecs. Cortés took La Malinche as a slave. La Malinche spoke both Spanish and the Aztec language of Nahuatl. She helped Cortés speak with Aztec leaders. She also had a son with him.

FACT

The film *The Curse of La Llorona* debuted in 2019. Cast members said they felt a ghostly presence on set.

Cortés took the Aztecs' land by force in 1521, ending the Aztec Empire. Some stories say that La Malinche felt guilty for helping Cortés. They say she spent her remaining days weeping over her betrayal of the Aztecs. Her weeping has been connected to the tale of La Llorona.

SKEPTIC'S NOTE

In reality, La Malinche married a Spanish man and had more children. No historical records support the idea that she spent her life in misery.

La Malinche was born with the name Malinal and has also been known as Malintzin and Doña Marina.

THE WEEPING WOMAN OF MEXICO

Tales of ghostly women in white aren't limited to Mexico and the southwestern United States. Different versions of these tales have been told around the world in many different cultures. Though the stories differ, they share many common threads. These ghosts often wear white but not always. They cry out to warn others of death or danger. People often tell these stories as a way to make sense of an uncertain world.

Most writers and scholars agree that La Llorona is an urban legend. Her story is used as a **cautionary** tale. Like most urban legends, it has many variations. In some, La Llorona weeps for the children she killed. In others, she is a beautiful woman who lures men to their deaths. No matter the story, the name La Llorona instills fear into everyone who hears it. So listen carefully the next time the sun goes down. You just might hear the weeping woman of Mexico.

MEDEA

The story of Medea from Greek mythology has a lot of similarities to the tale of La Llorona. Medea was a witch who was able to predict the future. She used her powers to help her husband, Jason, steal a sacred object from her father. Jason later left Medea for another woman. Like La Llorona, Medea killed her children. But she showed no **remorse** for their deaths.

According to legend, after killing her children, Medea later married Aegeus. She eventually attempted to poison his son, Theseus.

29

GLOSSARY

abduction (ab-DUHK-shuhn)—the action of taking someone away against his or her will

apparition (ap-uh-RISH-uhn)—the visible appearance of a ghost

Aztec (AZ-tek)—a member of an indigenous people who lived in Mexico before Spanish people settled there

barren (BARE-uhn)—often empty

bloodcurdling (BLUHD-kurd-ling)—causing terror or horror

cautionary (KAW-shun-air-ee)—careful or watchful

convent (KAHN-vent)—a building where a group of women who have devoted their lives to the church live

evidence (EV-i-duhns)—information and facts that help prove something is or is not true

familiar (fuh-MIL-yur)—an animal believed to be under the control of a witch or other magical being

highland (HYE-luhnd)—an area with mountains or hills

mythology (mith-AWL-uh-jee)—a group of old or ancient stories told again and again that help connect people with their past

peasant (PEZ-uhnt)—a poor person who owns a small farm or works on a farm

remorse (ri-MORS)—a strong feeling of guilt or regret over something done in the past

siren (SYE-ruhn)—half-bird, half-woman creature that lures sailors to their deaths by singing

skeptic (SKEP-tik)—someone who doubts or questions beliefs

sulfur (SUHL-fur)—a yellow chemical element found in gunpowder and matches that often smells like rotten eggs

widow (WID-oh)—a woman whose husband has died and who has not remarried

READ MORE

Coleman, Wim and Pat Perrin. *La Llorona: A Play Adapted from Mexican Folklore.* Setting the Stage for Fluency. South Egremont, MA: Red Chair Press, 2015.

Loh-Hagan, Virginia. *Vanishing Hitchhiker.* Urban Legends: Don't Read Alone! Ann Arbor, MI: Cherry Lake Publishing, 2018.

Peterson, Megan Cooley. *Haunting Urban Legends.* Scared! North Mankato, MN: Capstone Press, 2014.

INTERNET SITES

More Ghost Stories:
https://people.howstuffworks.com/culture-traditions/holidays-halloween/ghost-stories.htm

How Ghosts Work:
https://science.howstuffworks.com/science-vs-myth/afterlife/ghost.htm

Paranormal Technology:
https://www.npr.org/2011/10/31/141868232/paranormal-technology-gadgets-for-ghost-tracking

INDEX